空椅子

Empty Chairs

空椅子

Empty Chairs

詩選

Selected Poems

劉霞

Liu Xia

Translated from the Chinese
by Ming Di and Jennifer Stern

Foreword by Herta Müller and Introduction by Liao Yiwu

Graywolf Press

Some of these translations first appeared through the following organizations and in the
following publications:

PEN America, Chinese PEN, the BBC, the *Guardian,* the *Margins* (journal of the Asian
American Writers' Workshop), *Poetry, Poetry East West,* the Poetry Society of America,
and Words without Borders.

Liu Xia's photographs on the cover and interior were provided generously by Guy Sorman.
Liu Xia entrusted Guy Sorman with her original prints, which he smuggled out of China
and has shown in galleries around the world.

This publication is made possible, in part, by the voters of Minnesota through a Minnesota
State Arts Board Operating Support grant, thanks to a legislative appropriation from the arts
and cultural heritage fund, and through grants from the National Endowment for the Arts
and the Wells Fargo Foundation Minnesota. Significant support has also been provided by
Target, the McKnight Foundation, Amazon.com, and other generous contributions from
foundations, corporations, and individuals. To these organizations and individuals we offer
our heartfelt thanks.

ART WORKS.
arts.gov

MINNESOTA
STATE ARTS BOARD

CLEAN
WATER
LAND &
LEGACY
AMENDMENT

WELLS
FARGO

TARGET.

A Lannan Translation Selection
Funding the translation and publication of exceptional literary works

Published by Graywolf Press
250 Third Avenue North, Suite 600
Minneapolis, Minnesota 55401

www.graywolfpress.org

Published in the United States of America

ISBN 978-1-55597-725-2

2 4 6 8 9 7 5 3 1
First Graywolf Printing, 2015

Library of Congress Control Number: 2015939979

Cover design: Jeenee Lee Design

Cover art: Liu Xia

Contents

Foreword: A Mix of Silk and Iron

Liu Xia's poems are inevitably lyrical and inescapably documentary. They take her real life and put it on poetic record. Their sentences oppress, their images are both matter-of-fact and full of despair:

> When the show is over,
> I stay on stage with myself:
> one of me is tearful
> the other laughing loudly.

> Or: "I've been looted."
> Or: "My mind is filled with straw."
> Or: "You love your wife and are proud she stays with you."

Of course, we realize this woman is the wife of Liu Xiaobo, the Nobel laureate from China and that country's most famous political prisoner, now in his fifth year of his eleven-year sentence. His crime: the Charter 08 manifesto, which far from making aggressive demands offered measured, even cautious suggestions for converting China's communist, one-party system into a free and humane society. For that, he was given eleven years of prison, and his wife is subjected to constant surveillance, house arrest, isolation. Day in and day out she is unable to take a single step that goes unwatched. And this is the merciless substance of these poems, their point of departure.

Meanwhile, the regime is not content to torment Liu Xia alone for her husband's outspokenness, but has extended its retribution to other family members. To unsettle her further, they have arrested Liu Xia's brother on a ridiculously trumped-up charge. Despotism plain and simple.

In her poem "Snow," the author evokes her brother's birthday. I freeze on the inside when I read the sentence:

it must be hard to be my brother.

Out of this pain come the pangs of conscience, the creeping guilt, simply because nothing can be done about the groundless punishment this big state is inflicting on this small brother, this "little brother" who was born on the "Day of Great Snow." Simple contrasts on a steep poetic slope. Clear in their helplessness, lapidary but still tender. A quiet imploring is also a loud clamor. Liu Xia's poems are a mix of silk and iron. Because while iron political despotism rules outside, intimacy with all its hardships reigns within, the enigma of strong emotion.

Over and over we read about time, "the ladder of time."

Or: "Death from twenty years ago returns— / it comes and goes like time."

Here in these poems, time is exactly what it is in the everyday life of the author: stolen by the state. No matter how many details we examine, the longer we look at the particulars, we cannot escape the horrifying insight: the full length of stolen time is nothing less than stolen life.

Liu Xia's poetry is about self-assertion in a stolen life. Her poems possess a dignity that always manages to arise anew whenever it is battered down.

HERTA MÜLLER
Translated from the German by Philip Boehm

Introduction: The Story of a Bird

Liu Xia—the first poem of hers that filled me with wonder was "One Bird Then Another," written in May 1983. Recently, I was filled with grief, when I read her poem about a tree, "How It Stands," written in December 2013. Between the two poems, thirty years had passed.

What had happened in between?

When we first met, we were very young, and knew nothing but writing poetry. The bird called Liu Xia lived in a large cage-like room on the twenty-second floor of a building on West Double Elm Tree Lane in Beijing. I traveled from Sichuan to meet her and climbed up the stairs as the elevator was broken. From the moment I knocked on the cage door, Liu Xia never stopped giggling. Her chin became pointy when she smiled, and she laughed like a bird, unrestrained. No wonder she wrote this—

Then, we started to hate winter,
the long slumber.
We put a red lamp
outside overnight
so its light would tell our bird
we were waiting.

Even earlier than all this, in 1982, she sent me a poem about a small lamp by the Great Wall glittering in the vast darkness. The glittering was also, perhaps, the eyes of birds. In those days, Liu Xia had a portrait of the American poet Sylvia Plath above her bed. So we talked about Plath's three suicide attempts. The woman who could "eat men like air" played a game of death. What if she had died accidentally; what if there had been a gas leak; what if the gas repairman was just half an hour too late? Talking, we giggled for no good reason. Tears fell while we were still laughing. We were young, and we could laugh at death, whether we wanted to criticize it or praise it, we laughed and laughed, with wisdom or dementia, uncontrollably. Perhaps human beings should give up language, become birds and fly into the sky freely, stopping on trees to feed on insects when hungry—wouldn't that be enough?

But then in 1989, the violence at Tiananmen broke out, and many young people were killed. They might have, like us, at one point, laughed at death. Their souls climbed out of their bodies, which were perforated by bullets, like unseeable birds and flew before the eyes of Liu Xia and Liu Xiaobo. And so, through sleepless nights, the two were tied together, nested in each other's souls. Liu Xiaobo, despite having been jailed many times, continuously wrote poems and letters, clinging firmly to Liu Xia as his nest. This Nobel Peace Prize winner could tolerate the loss of freedom, but not spiritual solitude—I suppose it's man's nature. In a way, Liu Xia has been forced into being Liu Xiaobo's wife and his mother. They don't have children—which is the best way to live in a totalitarian country. Someone who goes to jail repeatedly relies on being taken care of inside and outside of the high walls.

Ten years ago, in my introduction to the *Selected Poems of Liu Xiaobo and Liu Xia*, I quoted the following lines:

Before you go into the grave
Don't forget to write to me with your ashes
Don't forget to leave your underworld address

I still think these are the best lines from Liu Xiaobo's poetry. But they are cruel, too cruel. Liu Xia's nature is to be an unrestrained bird. But because of the burden of his ruthless, extreme love, this bird that longs to fly has been imprisoned in a cage. In the old days, the cage was bigger; we were able to meet each other and laugh foolishly, unbridled. After hanging out with Liu Xia for a while, I could drink at her level, which made Xiaobo envious. In the winter of 2007, I wrote: "From the beginning, when I was just a little over twenty and had hardly ever tasted alcohol, Liu Xia was my drinking master. It was hard to measure how much she and her best friend, an unexpectedly good drinker as well, could consume. They both liked to laugh at men while they drank, ordering the famous Liu Xiaobo to open bottles for them. There were several times when Liu Xiaobo refused, pretending to be angry, but then he would be coerced back into the role of servant. He laughed, *hey-hey-hey-hey,* trying to please everybody, clumsily. When Liu Xiaobo's knowledge and education and his courage were completely torn apart, he would simply give up what he did best—writing articles and giving speeches. He would drink water at the liquor table, and sing popular songs from the 1980s, one after another. He sang so terribly, so off-key, and while he sang his throat hummed involuntarily, which made his listeners want to quit living. The more so, the louder he sang. And he had memorized the lyrics so perfectly. Before the sensational climax of a song, he would inhale, then exhale. He enjoyed himself. I forgot who said 'The best poem is one that makes pigs cry out.' I believe, pigs would scream if they heard Comrade Liu Xiaobo's songs."

Then, because of Charter 08, he went to jail for the fourth time. Then the Nobel Peace Prize. And then a deadly eleven-year prison sentence for Liu Hui, Liu Xia's brother, due to his so-called economic offenses but obviously due to his relationship with Liu Xiaobo. What's the matter with this country?

Liu Xia's burden has become too heavy. Her heart is beginning to fail. In isolation, she can only stare at a tree through her window, a tree that only a bird can dwell in:

Is it a tree?
It's me, alone.
Is it a winter tree?

It's always like this, all year round.

. . . . . .

Aren't you tired of being a tree your whole life?
Even when exhausted, I want to stand.
Is there anyone to keep you company?
There are birds.
I don't see any.

. . . . . .

I'm so old and blind I wouldn't see them.
You don't know how to draw a bird, do you?
You're right. I don't know how.
You're an old, foolish tree.
I am.

She is no longer the bird she once was, the one that flew high to Tibet, alone; the one that made circles around Lake Namtso, the mirror of heaven; the one that laughed until out of breath. Instead, she became a tree. She can't move her own nest—Liu Xiaobo can't move, so she can't either. She's turned from a bird into a tree, her feathers becoming white and withered. But as a tree she still sings the songs of birds.

When a bird is dying, her singing is sorrowful.

These are the only songs, the dying songs, of Chinese poetry since June 4th, 1989.

Escape, Liu Xia, I know you can.

If Liu Xiaobo learns about it from jail, he will support you—your change from a tree back into a bird.

LIAO YIWU
February 2014

空椅子

Empty Chairs

一隻鳥又一隻鳥

我們
在很早以前
就常常說起那隻鳥
不知道來自哪裡的鳥
我們興致勃勃
它給我們帶來了笑聲

冬天的一個晚上
是晚上，它真的來了
我們睡得很沉
誰也沒有看見它
就在有太陽的早晨
我們看見它留在玻璃上的
小小的影子
它印在那裡
好久不肯離去

我們討厭冬天了
討厭冬天長長的睡眠
我們想讓紅色的燈
長久地亮著
告訴那隻鳥
我們在等待

院裡的葡萄
又爬滿架子了
窗子不再關上
我們仍然記得那隻鳥
只是不再談起它

One Bird Then Another

Back then,
we were always talking
about the bird. Not knowing
where it came from—the bird,
the bird—it brought us
warmth and laughter.

One winter night—yes
it was a winter night—the bird
came to us while we were soundly
sleeping. Neither of us saw it.
In the morning we saw—sun on glass—
its small shadow
imprinted, staying
for a long time, refusing
to leave.

Then, we started to hate winter,
the long slumber.
We put a red lamp
outside overnight
so its light would tell our bird
we were waiting.

Vines full of grapes grew
in the yard. We kept the windows
open, remembering: the bird.
But we didn't talk
about it any more.

一個星期天
天陰沉沉的，沒有雨
我們一起出門了
去時裝店給我買了一件新衣服
天黑下來的時候，又去
那個人很多的餛飩舖子
一人吃了兩大碗餛飩
回來的路上
我們不吭聲了
心裡覺得有點不舒服

到家了
院子裡那盞燈忽明忽暗
一串青青的葡萄落在台階上
我們同時止住了步子
望了望天
又趕緊低下了頭
它來過了
可我們不敢說
只是在心裡想著
生怕它永遠不再來了

門終於開了
紅色的光神秘地鋪開
在有格子的紙上
你寫不出字了
我想試一試新衣服
卻怎麼也解不開扣子

它又來過了

5/1983

One Sunday, the sky was
overcast, but it wasn't raining.
We went out together and you bought
me a blouse from a boutique.
When it got dark, we went
to a crowded restaurant
and each ate two bowls of dumplings.
On the way back we
were quiet, not saying a word,
feeling slightly uneasy.

Arriving home, we saw
the lamp flickering in the yard
and a handful of green grapes on the porch.
We stopped walking
and looked up, then together
lowered our heads—
the bird had come and gone.
We murmured
but didn't speak, worried
it would never return.

The door opened at last
and a mysterious red radiance streamed out.
There was a piece of paper with written lines,
but you couldn't write a word.
I wanted to try on my new clothes
but I couldn't undress.

The bird, again, the bird.

5/1983

黑幡船

那個紅臉漢子捕走了你最喜歡的一條魚
一條黑色的魚懂得你心事的魚
你心欲裂把牙咬得咯咯響垂頭喪氣
你用手撫摸一下海面
手掠過的地方出現了無數條魚無數條魚
誘惑那紅臉漢子昇起船帆連夜出海
忘記這是在夜晚忘記會迷失方向

你悄悄地把那漢子拉進懷裡
一直到他的頭髮成為海草綠色的飄蕩
你平息了怒氣點支煙清煙縷縷
第二天，當鞭炮響起來
為滿黑幡的船開道的時候
你變成了一只眼睛一朵雲一陣風

那失去漢子的女人奶水一夜間消失了
你反覆托夢給那沒奶吃的孩子
說他的父親在海裡日子過得很快活很快活
那孩子長成了漢子整日一聲不吭
他甚麼都記得甚麼都不說

那女人生命的潮水遠遠退下去了
那叢綠色的海草隨浪搖動

12/1985

6

Black Sail

The ruddy man goes fishing and catches your favorite fish,
a black fish, a fish who knows you.
Your heart splits in pain, you clench your teeth in loss.
You stroke the sea, and where your hand touches, fish jump up—
so many fish. So many fish seduce the man to hoist the sail
and set out to sea for the night, forgetting
it's dark and one may lose the way.

You reach out your arms and pull the man
close, quiet, until his hair floats like seaweed.
Then you calm down and light a cigarette—green smoke
rises. The next day, when firecrackers
clear the way for a full black sail,
you become a gust of wind, a cloud, an eye.

The woman who lost the man loses her breast milk overnight.
You often appear in the dreams of that thirsty child,
telling him his father is happy in the sea. And he is happy.
The child grows into a man who keeps silent all day long.
He remembers everything but says nothing.

The woman's tide ebbs. The green seaweed fades
drifting away with each wave.

12/1985

日子

我們的生活
就像牆上這本掛曆
風景已經不再新鮮了

朋友們在夜晚到來
我會盡力做出一桌的菜
每道菜都不會忘記放鹽
不用喝酒
你的話就滔滔不絕
大家興高采烈
雞的腳指頭也啃得煞白

黎明時分
朋友們盤旋而去
燈光下
窗簾上的向日葵
依然豔麗而瘋狂
成堆的煙灰和美麗的魚骨
卡住了我們的喉嚨
我們相互不看一眼
就爬上床去

12/1986

Days

Our life, like the calendar
on the wall,
presents a stale picture.

Friends come at night
and I cook enough dishes to cover the table—
remembering to put salt in each.
You get chatty
without even drinking wine.
Everyone is happy and eats chicken feet
until the bones are sucked white.

At dawn, our friends are suddenly gone
like a breeze.
The sunflowers on the window curtain
are crazily bright
against the light.
Cigarette ashes and beautiful fish bones
are jammed down our throats.
Without looking at each other
we climb into bed.

12/1986

變形動物

你有一隻古裡古怪的動物
它有一只貓眼一只羊眼
從不與貓來往
還會突然攻擊羊群
有月亮的晚上
它在屋頂徜徉

你獨自一人的時候
它就趴在你的腿上
心事重重
長時間凝視你
露出一種挑戰的神氣

6/1988

Transformed Creature

You have a strange pet—
one eye is a cat's, the other a sheep's.
Yet, it won't socialize with felines,
will attack any flock of sheep.
On moonlit nights,
it wanders on roofs.

When you're alone,
it will lie in your lap,
preoccupied,
slowly studying you until—
on its face—a challenge.

6/1988

騙局

—給WB

你總是對我失望
我也對自己無可奈何

署著我姓名的詩歌在紙上
排列成行
可你並不知道這是一個騙局
那是一個寂寞的靈魂
偶爾來我筆下作客
他喜歡我的字跡
和我抽煙時的姿勢

我和他獨處的時候
我的字整齊又美麗
趁他走神的工夫
我給他喝下好多的白酒
想把他永久留下
他就是不肯上當

我真想放棄詩人的名譽
它讓人對我有太多的奢望
讓我時常面對白紙
絕望以致瘋狂

我想告訴世人事實真相
他就會突然出現
抓住我
我來不及歡喜
你來不及好好愛我
他便轉眼消失

Scheme

—for WB

You're always disappointed in me.
I too, can do nothing about myself.

Poems with my name
on them pile up,
but you don't know it's a scam.
A lonely soul, a guest,
comes now and then and moves my pen.
He likes my writing
and the way I smoke.

When I'm alone with him,
my words are tidy and beautiful.
When he's distracted,
I try to get him drunk
so he'll stay,
but he won't be fooled.

I want to give up my name as a poet.
It makes others expect things from me
and makes me face the blank page
with despair, and even madness.

I want to tell the world the truth,
but when I try, he appears
and seizes me.
Before I can revel
and before you can love me again
he is gone, instantly.

他的世界太大太遠
遠到今生今世
我不可能到達

我只能在這間屋子裡
當你平庸的老婆
買菜做飯洗衣服
或者點上一支香煙
長時間凝視窗外

只要我活著
就得聽任他擺佈

7/1988

His world is too far—
farther than I can reach
in this life.

I can only live in this room,
be your mediocre wife,
shop, cook, and do laundry,
or light a cigarette
and stare out the window for a long time.

My life—
I'm at his mercy.

7/1988

一九八九年六月二日

—給曉波

這不是個好天氣
我在茂盛的太陽底下
對自己說

站在你身後
拍了拍你的頭頂
頭髮直刺我手心
這種感覺有點陌生

我沒有來得及和你說上一句話
你成了新聞人物
和眾人一起仰視你
使我很疲倦
只好躲到人群外面
抽支煙
望著天

也可能此時正有神話誕生
然而陽光太耀眼
使我無法看到它

6/1989

June 2nd, 1989

—for Xiaobo

This isn't good weather
I said to myself
standing under the lush sun.

Standing behind you
I patted your head
and your hair pricked my palm
making it strange to me.

I didn't have a chance
to say a word before you became a character
in the news, everyone looking up to you
as I was worn down
at the edge of the crowd
just smoking
and watching the sky.

A new myth, maybe, was forming there,
but the sun's sharp light
blinded me from seeing it.

6/1989

遊戲

—給自己

我盤腿坐在這裡
點燃一支香煙
頭腦清醒得如同上帝

我看到另一個自己
在人間玩一場危險的遊戲

你穿著戲裝
玩得那麼開心
戲中的你無拘無束
我以各種方式提醒你
千萬不可太隨意

我讓你在夢中驚醒
在你上樓梯時滅掉所有的燈
你沒有帶傘的那天
突降一場大雨

可以全不在意
像個忘乎所以的孩子
一心一意進行那場遊戲

我真羨慕你
不是這個頭腦清醒的上帝

Game

—for myself

Sitting here cross-legged,
lucid as a God,
I light a cigarette.

I see another me playing a dangerous
game in the human world.

You're enjoying yourself,
wearing a costume, acting
whimsical. I try to remind you
every way I can
not to be careless.

I startle you while you're sleeping,
snuff out the lights as you're walking upstairs.
If you don't have an umbrella,
I pour heavy rain.

But you don't mind in the least,
like a child carried away with herself.
You play your games wholeheartedly.

I envy your not being
a clear-headed God.

給我一杯酒
讓我和你一起遊戲
管它結局是滿堂喝采
還是獨自一人
在夜晚哭泣

12/1992

Give me a glass of wine.
Let me play the game with you
regardless of ending with a full house applauding
or one person alone crying
to the night.

12/1992

一個詞

某天早晨
一個詞
好像一個陰謀
躲在別人的夢中窺視著我
就在我睜開眼睛的一瞬間
它以優雅的姿態
佔據了我

孤單的詞
如同絕症
疼痛並且尖利
可以置人於死地

我真羨慕這個詞
佔有了我
然後生機勃勃

6/28/1995

Word

In the morning, a word
from someone else's dream
peeks at me
like a conspiracy.
The minute I open my eyes
the word, with an elegant gesture,
takes me.

The lonely word
like an incurable disease
causes pain, screaming,
and possibly death.

But I'm envious—
it flies up when it
takes me.

6/28/1995

我坐在這裡

我坐在這裡
看天色由明到暗
傾聽最後一縷陽光
發出呻吟
等待第一滴淚
敲響敞開的窗戶玻璃

一個詞等待另一個詞
永不相遇
一滴雨
使天地渾然一體
在靜止的時間裡
雨的靈魂
悄悄地降臨

6/1995

I Sit Here

I sit here
watching the sky go
from light to dark,
listening to the last of the sun
groan, waiting for the first drop to
knock on the open window.

One word waiting for another—
they will never meet.
A drop of rain
makes the sky and earth one piece.
In stilled time,
the soul of rain
quietly comes down.

6/1995

毒藥

梵高的耳朵傳遞給我
緊張如大地就要崩潰的消息

警惕那些天空如洗的夜晚
餐桌中央怒放的鮮花
書本裡有序的語句
電視台關於氣候的消息
卡夫卡眼睛的瘋狂

守護最後一縷爐火
如同天災後農人守護
地裡唯一一穗高粱

我是這個世界的毒藥
看見白雪覆蓋下
大地正在腐爛的屍體
屍體上蠕動的蛆
別想用純潔來欺騙我

不要掩藏死亡
不要人造的天堂
偽天使們熱烈的目光
不如一根枯黃的稻草
一隻香煙燃盡的輝煌

1/1997

Poison

Van Gogh's ear sends me an urgent message
that the earth is about to collapse.

Beware of the white-washed night sky
the flowers in full bloom on the dining room table
the orderly lines of sentences in a book
the weather forecast on TV
and Kafka's crazy eyes.

Guard the last ray of fire
like farmers guarding the only sorghum
left in a field after a natural disaster.

I am the poison of this world.
I can see a rotting corpse, the earth,
covered in snow
and I can see wriggling maggots.
Do not try to fool me with purity.

Do not hide death.
Do not build an artificial paradise.
The warm look from the eyes of a fake angel
is worse than the glory of straw yellowing
or a cigarette burning out.

1/1997

外祖父

落滿灰塵的向家祠堂
一片恍惚的陰影
徘徊不去
是你嗎? 我面容模糊的外祖父
多少年了, 我透過近視的雙眼
尋找你的手
觸摸我不曾走動過的歲月
在夢中回到你的家園

我知道你存在
舊照片上你發黃的青春
與這南方持久的碧綠
相距實在太遠

獨自一人時
我常常看到
你牽著我的手
我們一起走在一本又一本書中
心中充滿悲涼
沒有人告訴過我
關於你的任何一個微小的細節
似乎你生活在冰川期以前
而我又無力成為考古學家

我只能用心
把你交還給這些
單薄的詞語
你在陳舊的老宅裡
是否感到了一縷
新鮮的空氣
外祖父

2/1997

Grandfather

In the dusty ancestral hall,
a lingering shadow
doesn't want to leave.
Is that blurred face you, grandfather?
For years, through my myopic
eyes, I've tried to seek your hands, to touch
the years I had never passed through.
In dreams, only, I arrive at your house.

I know you exist.
Your yellowed youth in old photos
looks alien in this
southern green.

When I'm alone, I often see you
holding my hand. Together
we walk through book
after book,
which fills me with chilling grief.
Nobody shares the details
of your life, as if you lived
before the ice age. It's impossible
for me to become an archaeologist.

I can only put my whole self
into giving you back
to these thin, frail words.
In your old house, do you feel
a flash
of fresh air,
grandfather?

2/1997

一個人的風景

一個人的風景
在過路人的眼裡
單調並且荒涼
如同遺忘在辭海裡的一個字
破碎的鏡片上殘缺的影像

學會閉上眼睛繪畫
用靈魂聲援
每一個筆觸每一點明亮

盲人的風景
因為一顆心而
無拘無束

在監禁中
你能夠到達
耶路撒冷那面哭牆

4/1997

A Landscape

One person's landscape
is monotonous and desolate
in the eyes of passersby,
like a forgotten word in the ocean of a dictionary,
an incomplete image in a broken lens.

With my eyes closed, I learn how to paint
by myself and in solidarity with you in my soul,
brighter with every stroke.

A blind person's landscape,
as it's of one heart and mind,
is unfettered, unrestrained.

Even when imprisoned
you can reach
the Wailing Wall in Jerusalem.

4/1997

陰影

—給曉波

某個早晨我在睡眠之中
陰影如夢境游移不定
至今仍阻擋我的視線
時間流逝季節更替
而那個漫長又殘忍的早晨
沒有結局

一把椅子一隻煙斗
在記憶裡徒勞地把你等待
誰也看不見走在街角的你
眼睛裡飛翔著一隻鳥
一顆青果倒在無葉的樹上
經歷了秋天的那個早晨
它拒絕成熟

一個目光炯炯的女人
開始夜以繼日地書寫
連綿不斷的囈語
鏡中之鳥依然沈睡

4/1997

Shadow

—for Xiaobo

One morning as I was sleeping,
a shadow hovered over me like a dream.
This shadow still blocks my vision.
Time goes by, seasons change,
but that long, cruel morning
hasn't ended.

A chair and a pipe
wait for you in vain.
No one sees you walking down the street.
In your eyes, a bird is flying,
green fruit hangs from a tree without leaves—
since that morning, the fruit refuses
to ripen in the fall.

A woman with burning eyes
starts writing day and night
with endless dream-words while the bird
in the mirror falls into a deep sleep.

4/1997

某個夜晚

一根針掉進那夜晚
器官迸裂
柔軟清夜
在意外的疼痛之中
面部痙攣

一個女人坐在檯燈前
坐在睡眠之外
雙手在空中絕望地揮舞
纖細的手指間空空蕩蕩
所有關於黑暗的詞彙
四下奔逃
手的影子投射到牆上
變形如剪紙

只有心頭那隻不眠的貓
在血中悲鳴
目光雪亮

和虛無作戰的女人
連同語言
最終被她指間的黑暗吞沒

那顆叫做「波普」的彗星
在夜空上
神秘地飛行

4/9/1997

One Night

A needle fell into the night.
Organs split.
During that soft, clear night,
unexpected pain
caused facial spasms.

A woman sat by the lamp
outside of her sleep desperately
waving her hands in the air.
Emptiness slipped between
her slender fingers.
All the words about darkness fled,
as her hands projected shadows on the wall
then deformed like cut paper.

Only the sleepless cat inside her
cried out in her blood, its eyes beaming
like snow.

The woman fighting nothing,
in the end, was engulfed with her words by
the nothing between her fingers.

A comet called Hale-Bopp
flew mystery across
the night sky.

4/9/1997

驚醒的時候

驚醒的時候
四周一片漆黑
那隻鳥再次在我的手心裡尖叫
無數隻腳踏著樓梯
整座樓搖搖欲墜

我獨自坐在床上
手緊緊的握成拳頭
在冰涼的膝上一動不動
尖叫聲喘息著掙扎著
在拳頭中間

夢中到達的地方
一定危機重重
它離我很近
就是在鳥的尖叫聲中
我也能聽到它的呼吸

你在時間的反面
站在明亮的陽光下
看著一片羽毛
隨風飄落

4/18/1997

Awakened

When I woke up,
I was surrounded by the dark.
The bird in my palm screamed again,
then came the sound of footsteps on the stairs.
The building was about to fall down.

I sat alone in bed,
hands gripped into fists
on my cold knees.
Screams gasped for breath, struggled in
my tight fists.

I had come to that moment
in a dream when a crisis
is closing in.
Within the screaming, I could hear
the bird's breath.

But you were on the opposite side
of time, standing in the sunlight
watching a feather
drift down the wind.

4/18/1997

黯夜

那些眼睛今夜會回來
那些幽靈今夜會回來
以墓碑的姿態

那個時辰把自己固定在我心裡
即便記憶充滿枯草

空蕩蕩的墓地
沒有向日葵低垂
沒有梵高瘋狂的道別
悲痛的白骨
大地深處的冰河

所有幽靈所有的眼睛
聚集在這點燭火旁
用沈默與我對話
白色的百合花
難以覺察地開始凋落

生與死不可比較
真實和虛構
如同手心手背
這個從未結束的夜晚
一滴淚的想像之樹
掛滿絕望之手

在你的黑暗之夜
我的詞彙難以成形

Dark Night

Those eyes will return tonight
with their ghosts
in the shape of tombstones.

One moment stays in my mind
even though my mind is filled with straw.

The empty tomb
doesn't have a drooping sunflower,
or any of van Gogh's mad good-byes.
Bones are grieving:
an icy riverbed deep in the earth.

All the ghosts with all those eyes
are gathering here by the candle
speaking to me in a silent dialogue.
The white white lilies
start to fall, unnoticed.

I can't compare life with death,
truth with fabrications,
my palms with the back of my hands.
Tonight, the night that never ends,
a tree grows out of tear, and from the tree
many desperate hands are hanging.

In your dark night
my words fail to form.

我們無法回到
回到那個時辰
只有風
遊蕩在十里長街

穿過這個黑暗之夜的女人
百合花也不願令她佇足
她帶著寫滿詩歌的本子
她唯一的行囊
跟隨幽靈們的腳步

一頁頁白紙
在夜晚的視線之外飄飛

6/3-4/1997

We can't return
to that moment.
Only wind wanders down
the Long Street of Eternal Peace.

A woman passes through the dark night,
white lilies refuse to stop her.
She carries a notebook filled with poems,
the one thing she's brought,
and follows the footsteps of ghosts.

Into the night leaf after leaf
of white paper flies beyond sight.

6/3–4/1997

卡夫卡

卡夫卡
不知從什麼時候起
你不再是獨自一人
走在布拉格的天空下

轉瞬之間
冒出你的無數兄弟

在我的出生地
曾經萬眾一心眾口一詞服從統一
現在又有眾多手臂舉起
以你的名義
一起向城堡進軍

卡夫卡
你成為另一種意義的上帝
在虛假的前提下
他們褻瀆著城堡
自覺地把自己打扮成殉道者

卡夫卡
我看見你在尋找城堡的路上
腳步開始遲疑

還是讓我們回到老光棍
布魯姆菲爾德的家裡
你忘了嗎
這個故事還沒有結局

Kafka

Kafka—
I don't know how long it's been
since you walked alone
under the Prague sky.

All of a sudden, your brothers
appear—throngs of them.

Where I was born,
we would collectively follow orders
and now there are people raising
their arms in your name,
marching to the castle.

Kafka—
you've become a new kind of god.
They've desecrated the castle
with a false premise
and pretend to be martyrs.

Kafka—
I see you searching for the road to the castle
but also hesitating.

Let us return to the Elderly Bachelor
Blumfeld's house then.
Have you forgotten that this story
has no ending?

我們一起轉過身
看看那兩只
會自己跳動的小球
在哪裡

6/1997

Let us turn around
to see where the two balls
bounce endlessly
of their own accord.

6/1997

一個母親

只能用仇視我
來表達她對兒子衰老的愛

她想重新把那個倔強的兒子
放回早已乾枯的子宮
她口中喋喋不休的道理
難以說服那顆會飛的頭腦
她多次習慣性地舉起皮帶
抽到的只有虛空

她滿腔憤怒地
把玩著手中的麵團
隨時有可能
擊中我

10/1997

A Mother

Only by hating me
can she show her aging love for her son.

She wants to take that stubborn son
back into her dry womb.
Her mouth goes on and on spouting arguments
that can't change his flighty mind.
She keeps raising a belt out of habit
but only beats the void.

Filled with anger,
she toys with the dough in her hands
and, at any moment, might
smack me.

10/1997

黃昏

我喜愛這個時刻
黃昏降臨
周圍的一切事物
在曖昧的光線裡
千姿百態
正午的陽光
深夜寂靜的淚水
都不曾如此豐富如此
游移不定

街燈還沒有點亮
殘陽嬰兒般柔弱
刻骨的等待在這個時候
似乎也有些漫不經心

我坐在這瞬間的遲緩之中
從容地抽完天黑以前
最後一支香煙
越來越大的陰影
沈甸甸壓過來
詞語在渾沌中碎裂

表象之外
那隻鳥在飛
高高在上

4/1998

Twilight

I like this moment.
Dusk is falling.
Everything around me
dances in uncertain light.
The midday sun
and midnight tears—
silent, neither have been
so colorful
as they wander around me.

The streetlights are unlit.
The setting sun is baby-soft.
This long hour of waiting—deep
in one's bones—feels casual.

I sit in the slowness of this swift moment,
calmly smoking the last cigarette
before dark.
Growing shadows press heavily
overhead. Words break apart
in the midst of chaos.

Beyond and above all of this
a bird is flying
high.

4/1998

沒有人看見我

沒有人看見我
無可奈何
我並沒有受到過任何詛咒
只是被不容易得到的東西吸引
被拒絕我的東西吸引
被現實以外的東西吸引

日常生活使我貧乏
我相信那種
荒誕的幻想的瘋狂的真正的生活
躲在死人的面具後面
躲在厚厚的影子後面
我為我的想法哭泣
它們在屋子裏
就地旋轉

我看見行走在死亡線上的影子
邁著緩慢而又節奏的步子
從容不迫
沒有人說一句話
我做了一個手勢
沒有人看見我

5/1998

Nobody Sees Me

Nobody sees me
helpless.
I'm not being cursed. I'm just easily
attracted to unattainable things—
things that reject me,
that are outside what's real.

My life steals from me.
I believe in a life that is an absurd
fantasy and is also hyperreal,
a life that hides behind death masks
and looming shadows.
I cry out to my own thoughts
that are spinning
on the floor.

I see a shadow walking on death's path—
slowly, rhythmically,
calmly. Nobody
speaks a word.
I wave—nobody
sees me.

5/1998

混亂

瑪格麗特・杜拉斯
她選中了我
把我拉下時間的階梯
結束了我獨往獨來的生活
我無法再滿足觀看
日常生活的表象
渴望頭腦被痛擊

真正的混亂佔據了我
我被虛幻包圍了
到處是陌生的影子
陷阱叢生
我不再是這個房間的主人
我被掠奪一空
莒哈絲在酒後的瘋狂裡
呼風喚雨

如果有甚麼要毀滅
請不要留下痕跡

應該有一隻手
揭示
至今還沒有表現出來的東西
簡單而堅決

5/1998

Chaos

Marguerite Duras
has chosen me.
She's pulled me off the ladder of time,
ending my days of moving through on my own.
I'm no longer satisfied merely watching
the surface of my daily life.
I want to be tapped on the head and feel pain.

Real chaos occupies me—
I'm surrounded by unreal images.
Strange shadows are everywhere
and everywhere there are traps.
I'm no longer the owner of this room.
I've been looted.
Duras orders me around
in her drunken madness.

If something is to be destroyed
please don't leave traces behind.

There should be a hand
to give a simple
but firm signal
for anything that's not yet clear.

5/1998

錯位

在毫無防備的脆弱時刻
一齣沒有綵排過的戲上演了

我被耀眼的燈光出賣
我看到自己站在台上
荒唐的姿態
愚人的尖牙齒閃閃發光

原本悲哀並且柔弱的角色
失去了控制
飢餓了很久的血管
突然就大浪滔滔
我變成了邪惡的紅眼睛巫婆
眾目睽睽下
用骷髏製著美酒

任何戲裝和脂粉
難以將我偽裝

曲終人散
我和我並肩站在台上
一個淚流滿面
一個放聲大笑

7/1998

Misplaced

Fragile and unprepared, I've been tossed
into a play with no dress rehearsal.

Betrayed by the shimmering lights,
I see myself standing on the stage
in an absurd posture; I see
the fool's sharp teeth gleaming.

The character, assumed
sad and weak,
loses control: her hungry veins
burst into surging waves.
So I become a red-eyed evil witch,
and, under watchful eyes,
brew wine inside skulls.

No costume or makeup
can disguise me.

When the show is over,
I stay on stage with myself:
one of me is tearful
the other laughing loudly.

7/1998

空椅子

空椅子空椅子
如此之多的空椅子
在世界各處
梵高畫中的空椅子格外誘人

我悄然坐上去
試圖搖晃一下雙腿
椅子裡滲出的氣息
凍僵了它們
一動也不能動

梵高揮舞著手中的畫筆
離開離開離開
今夜沒有葬禮

梵高直直逼視我的目光
讓我垂下眼簾
如一隻有待燒製的陶器
坐在向日葵的烈焰之中

8/1998

Empty Chairs

Empty empty empty
so many empty chairs
everywhere. They look
charming in van Gogh's paintings.

I sit quietly on them
and try to rock
but they don't move—
they are frozen
by what's breathing inside.

Van Gogh waves his paintbrush—
leave leave leave
there's no funeral tonight.

He looks straight through me,
and I sit down
in the flames of his sunflowers
like a piece of clay to be fired.

8/1998

給林昭

我就這樣
久久地注視你的眼睛
輕輕地取出你嘴裡的棉團
你的嘴唇依然柔軟
你的墳墓空空蕩蕩
你的血燙傷了我伸出的手
如此寒冷又殘酷的死亡
讓九月燦爛陽光中獨坐的我
無法悲傷

任何形式的墓地
於熱愛自由的你
都過於輕浮

每年的陰曆十五
河上會佈滿河燈
卻招不回你的靈魂
你冷眼端坐在
卡夫卡筆下四處漂流的冥船上
看這個世界依然荒唐
北大百年校慶的舉杯歡呼
讓你冷冷大笑

喝吧喝吧喝吧
這是血呢
你在黑暗中說

9/1998

To Lin Zhao

Like this, I look into your eyes,
and keep looking while
I gently take the cotton out of your mouth.
Your lips are still soft,
your tomb is empty,
your blood burns my outstretched hands.
Death, cold and cruel, makes me sit alone
in the September sun,
incapable of feeling sad.

Any kind of tomb
will seem frivolous
to freedom-loving you.

Mid-autumn, every year,
lanterns float on the river,
but they can't call your soul back.
Your eyes cold, you sit
on the nether-boat that sails under Kafka's pen
looking out at the absurd world.
The toasts for the centennial of Peking University
make you laugh and sneer.

Drink drink drink,
this is blood—
you say in the darkness.

9/1998

沈默的力量

和玩偶們一起生活
沈默的力量無所不在
世界四面敞開
我們在手勢中交流
陰影裡，那個假想的紅蘋果
在寂靜中散發著幽香
不要開口
幻象會轉眼消失

黑暗總是不分時間
降臨在我週圍
一個玩偶背對著我
長時間凝視窗外
大雪耀眼的白色
刺痛了她的雙眼
可她堅持不肯閉上眼睛
愛如此簡單又如此艱難

我被這一景象感動
越來越沈默寡言
必須好好守護這些
薄而易碎的東西
一如我們的生活

11/1998

Silent Strength

Living with dolls, the power
of silence is omnipresent.
The world opens in four directions,
and we communicate with gestures.
In the shadows, in silence, an imaginary
red apple exudes a fragrance.
Do not open your mouth or the illusion
will disappear in the blink of an eye.

Darkness constantly falls around me
regardless of the time.
A doll turns her back to me
to stare out the window for a while.
The dazzling white of the snow
stings her eyes,
but she refuses to close them.
Love is so simple yet so difficult.

I'm moved by her
and my silence deepens.
I must guard these
small fragile things
as if guarding our life.

11/1998

無語

一次次在記憶中找出那些鞋
試圖給玩偶們穿上
鞋對玩偶們來說
太大太重了
鞋子的主人們在照片裡
無言地將我注視
我成為一段燃燒的木頭
就是給我地球上所有的海水
我也拒絕漂浮

有甚麼力量能夠橫空出世
讓時光倒轉
我呆呆凝望
那最後的時刻

猶太孩子們
臨死前寫下的詩句
在我反覆的默唸中
銘刻在我身體的每一根骨頭上

在這些空空蕩蕩的鞋子中間
我的骨頭
正在穿破皮肉
那些裸露的小腳
冰涼

1/1999

Speechless

Over and over I hunt for shoes
inside my memory, shoes
to put on the dolls
but the ones I find are too big and heavy.
The owners of the shoes look back at me
from photographs, silent.
I become a piece of burning wood.
Give me all the water on earth,
and I will still refuse to float.

Is there a force somewhere in the sky
that can turn the clock back?
I stare blankly, wait
for the final moment.

There were Jewish children
who wrote poems before dying.
In silent recitation,
I carve lines on my bones.

Inside empty shoes
my bones
are piercing flesh and skin,
those bare feet
ice-cold.

1/1999

正午

一個已經開始衰老的女人
推著一輛童車
走在充滿陽光和塵土的公園裡
童車裡端坐著一些玩偶

孩子們鬆開大人們的手
從四處奔跑而來
女人的腳步輕柔
玩偶們寂靜無聲
孩子們卻神奇地聽到了
正午的呼喚
他們跌跌撞撞地跟隨在童車旁
不時看看車裡的玩偶
又抬頭看看推車的女人

大人們遠遠地注視著
這支隊伍
大聲喊叫自己的孩子
然而所有的聲音
都消失在陽光和塵土之間

那個女人
步伐沈著而堅定
沒有人知道
她是誰
她要到哪裡去

2/1999

High Noon

An aging woman is pushing
a baby stroller
through a park of sun and dust.
Some dolls sit upright in the stroller.

Children free themselves from their parents' hands
and run closer from across the park.
The woman walks gently
and the dolls are silent,
but strangely the children can hear
high noon crying.
They stumble and follow the stroller,
looking back and forth from the dolls
to the woman who's pushing them.

The parents are watching the parade
from a distance;
they call their children's names
but their voices are lost
between the sun and dust.

The woman walks
calmly, her pace is steady.
No one knows
who she is
or where she's heading.

2/1999

只是醒來而已

我寄居在玩偶們的身體裡
一次次在夢中殺死自己
醒來的時候
卻發現自己並沒有再生
只是醒來而已

有時候在人們面前
我臉上出現一種
甚麼也不在乎的表情
那種蠻橫的神態
讓自己都以為
我已經頓悟了一切
沒有人知道
夜晚孤燈下枯坐的我
多麼愧疚
又是怎樣地
心懷感激

風已經吹動了窗簾
誰又能肯定
它僅僅是風呢

9/12/1999

It's Only Waking Up

I live in the bodies of the dolls
who kill themselves over and over in dreams.
When I wake up
I find myself not reborn
but only waking up.

Sometimes in front of other people
I wear an I-don't-care
expression,
the kind of arrogant face
that makes me feel like
I've had an epiphany.
No one knows
that I sit alone with a single light at night
feeling guilty
and grateful
at the same time.

Wind has been blowing the curtains,
but who can prove
it's just the wind?

9/12/1999

柚子

我把玩著一個又大又圓的柚子
金黃的一團
散發著苦澀的清香
用一把小刀
就能劃破它看似很厚的表皮
在無言的疼痛之中
我開始顫慄

感覺不到疼痛的生活
如同無人採摘的果實
等待它的只有腐爛腐爛

我真想成為這隻柚子
被刀切被手剝被牙咬
寧肯在疼痛中
安詳地死去
也不願看到自己正在腐爛的肉體
長滿了蠕動的蛆

整整一個冬天
我都會重複著同樣的事情
把一隻隻柚子剝開
在死亡中汲取營養

9/13/1999

A Grapefruit

I'm holding a big round
golden grapefruit
that smells bitter. A small knife
can cut through what seems
to be thick skin—
I'm starting to shiver
in quiet pain.

A life without pain
is an unpicked
fruit: it rots.

I want to be a grapefruit
cut by a knife or bitten apart.
I'd rather be in pain
and die in pain peacefully
than watch my body rot
with maggots squirming inside.

This whole winter
I've been doing one thing repeatedly—
peeling grapefruits one after another
absorbing the nutrients of my own death.

9/13/1999

靈魂是紙做的

—給曉波

在時間的黑夜中誕生
並不關注死後
有甚麼等待著我
早在一千年前
我就在世了
如此久遠駭人聽聞

世間總有令人驚詫的東西
一個生物越具有魔性
就越應該展示

我不是個瘋子
一切都是徵兆
一束光反射到手上
旋即消失
擺脫那滯留於此的
種種平庸

不斷觀察難解的符號
某些聲音在我耳邊
模糊不清

永遠是孤兒
拒絕出生的孩子
緊趴在我的手上
每次試圖把他拉開
他便抽搐
蜷縮進手心

A Soul Made of Paper

—for Xiaobo

Born in the dark hours,
I'm not concerned with what's waiting
for me after death.
I've already lived
a thousand years, long enough
to shock you.

There's always something surprising
in this world. The more magical a creature is,
the more it should display its strangeness.

I'm not a madwoman.
Everything is a sign.
A beam of light reflects off my hands,
then instantly disappears,
getting rid of what stands here,
the various mediocre details.

I observe all obtuse symbols
and hear a voice in my ear—
indistinct.

The perpetual orphan,
the child who refused to be born,
he clings to my hands, tight.
Each time I try to push him away,
he twitches and curls
in my palm.

有時
他也會用力一蹬
飛向群星

沉湎於兒時
那首荒唐而單調的歌
悲傷已經麻木
老鼠退回洞穴
我發現了
一個異常的現象
人們行走時總向地面
傾斜

他們正在變成動物
哈哈! 人的靈魂
是紙做的

7/8/2000

Sometimes, though,
he stretches forcefully
and flies to the stars.

I indulge in singing absurd
and monotonous songs from childhood,
and my sadness numbs.
Mice return to their cave
and I discover a strange
phenomenon: people walk
toward the ground
tilted.

They are turning into animals.
Ha ha! The human soul
is made of paper.

7/8/2000

無法擺脫

—給曉波

你剛剛上了火車
我就開始等待在電話旁
心中充滿焦慮
有些東西無法擺脫

你突然消失的陰影
遠遠沒有退去
以至你任何一次出行
都讓我
緊張不已

總是在睡夢中
看到你在
我無法辨認的地方
你不知道怎樣回家
我害怕

我必須要每天晚上
聽到你的聲音
在恐怖之車到來之前
咬碎你說出的每一個字

這是一種病

7/29/2000

Entrapped

—for Xiaobo

As soon as you got on the train,
I started waiting by the phone, filled
with anxiety. There are things
I can't escape.

You disappeared suddenly,
leaving behind a shadow that
lingered.
Each time, your departure
made me nervous.

While sleeping, I'd see you
in places
I couldn't recognize.
You'd lose your way home,
which filled me with dread.

Every night I needed
to hear your voice.
Before the arrival of that terrifying train,
I chewed and swallowed every word you uttered.

This is a disease.

7/29/2000

月亮中的殺人故事

這個晚上
有人驅車趕到郊外的寺廟
有人在房頂喝酒
有人啃著甜膩膩的月餅
望著天傻笑
有嬰兒貓一般哭叫
有人在電話裡客氣地問好
所有的人都以為
今夜和往日不一樣
月亮又大又圓在天上

我在燈下
讀一本殺人故事

一個男人
用了兩天時間
殺死了
妻子、一雙兒女、父親母親
還有一隻貓

一切發生以後
人們發現他從來就不是
他們認識的那個
面容和善的朋友
他的生活除了謊言還是
謊言
他活著並且在他六十一歲時出獄

Murder under the Moon

Tonight
some people are driving to temples on the outskirts
of the city, some are drinking on roofs.
Some, gnawing on sweet, greasy mooncakes,
look up at the sky and laugh.
Babies are howling.
Some people are saying "hello" politely
on the phone. Everyone thinks tonight
is not a regular night.
The moon is big and round up there.

I'm reading a murder story
under a light.

A man,
in two days,
killed
his wife, son, and daughter; his father and mother;
and a cat.

And then
people discovered he'd never been
the one they knew,
kind and friendly.
His life—one lie and another.
He's still alive and will
get out of prison when he's sixty-one.

他在獄中參加了
「不間斷者」組織
每月用兩個小時在凌晨祈禱
他以上帝為理由
感到巨大的寧靜
沐浴在光明之中

我必須盡可能快的讀完
我的血就要凍住了
凌晨已到
祈禱聲中
我變成了死去孩子的眼睛
月亮在我視線裡
越來越小

我的心被放置在玻璃瓶子裡
不蹦也不跳

In prison he joined
a group named "Uninterrupted."
Two mornings for two hours each month
he prays in the name of God
and feels a great serenity,
as if bathed in light.

I must finish as quickly as I can.
My blood is about to freeze.
Morning has come.
In a spoken prayer,
I become a dead child's eyes.
The moon grows smaller
and smaller in my gaze.

My heart has been placed in a glass bottle
and now it doesn't jump or beat, not even a bit.

月光下的骷髏

戰爭要結束前夕
一顆砲彈落進院子
她看見媽媽在爆炸聲中
躺倒在地
內臟露了出來
懷裡的娃娃和她一樣
全身血紅
她的眼睛張開
並且含著淚水

他在坑底放了一塊毯子
讓媽媽躺在上面
那個娃娃始終抱在胸前
他用另一塊毯子把她們蓋上
把坑填滿

爸爸到來的時候
外面下著雨
爸爸問起他的媽媽
泥土被再次翻開
一具大骷髏的胸前
還有一具小小的骷髏
爸爸看著看著
臉上濕成一片
不知是淚水還是雨水
爸爸爬出墓穴
頭也不回地走了

他把那些骨頭搬到閣樓
在草墊上攤開
讓骨頭快些晾乾
沒有屍體的墓穴再次填滿

Moonlit Skeletons

Before the war ended
a bomb fell on the yard,
and he saw his mother fall to the ground
from the blast,
her internal organs exposed.
The doll in her arms was red with blood,
like its mother, its eyes
were open, filled
with tears.

He put a blanket underneath
his mother in the pit,
the doll still in her arms.
He put a blanket over them
and filled the hole.

When his father came home,
it was raining.
He asked about his mother.
They dug in the soil and uncovered
a large skeleton
with a small skeleton in its arms.
The father stood looking,
his face wet
with tears or rain, it wasn't clear.
He climbed out of the grave,
and left.

The boy moved the bones to the attic
and spread them out on mats
to dry. The empty grave
was filled again with soil.

幾個月以後
他把媽媽和娃娃的骨頭
擦淨磨亮
小心翼翼地用細鐵絲
串起每根骨頭

時常在失眠的夜晚
我看見
月光照亮遙遠的閣樓
母親和娃娃的骷髏
還掛在梁柱上
左右晃動

骷髏下
那個日漸蒼老的男孩
蜷曲著熟睡
死亡在他之上

11/16/2000

A few months later,
he wiped and polished
the big bones and the small bones,
and strung them carefully
on a thin wire.

During my sleepless nights
I often see
the moonlit attic in the distance—
the skeletons of the mother and doll
hanging from the beams, swinging
back and forth.

Underneath the skeletons
an aging boy
curls up in sleep
while death hangs above.

11/16/2000

結尾

—給曉波的母親

你突然走了
從發病進醫院
到咽下最後一口氣
僅僅兩個小時
這是你一直渴望的死法
你做到了，媽媽
留下我們在血中窒息

電話傳來你入院的消息
我們正在和朋友們喝酒
我在念詩人凱文・哈特寫的
《為死者祈禱》

在殯儀館我最後一次見到你
你是那麼的小
穿著嶄新的衣服
臉上塗著厚厚的胭脂
我害怕你變成我鏡頭裡
怨靈附體的娃娃
我想逃跑
曉波緊緊抓住我的手
我一動也不能動

The End

—for Xiaobo's mother

Suddenly, you're gone.
Two hours after entering
the hospital you took
your last breath.
This is the way you longed to die.
You did it, mother,
leaving us choking on blood.

When the call came with the news
we were drinking with friends,
and I was reading a poem by Kevin Hart
called "Praying for the Dead."

I saw you for the last time at the funeral home.
You seemed tiny in the new clothes,
your face caked with makeup.
I was afraid you would turn into a doll,
one of the dolls possessed by rage
in my photographs.
I wanted to run out
but Xiaobo took my hand firmly.
I couldn't even move.

媽媽
我知道你從來就不喜歡我
你一直懷疑
你兒子的下獄
你兒子不肯回大連跟你一起生活
以至你每一次生病
全是我這個壞女人一手策畫的
你特別不能容忍我的笑
你讓我滾出去

第一次進你的家
屋裡到處都是塑料布和塑料袋子
沙發床墊地毯暖氣抽屜
甚至連切菜板水壺
全被各種塑料包裹塞滿
我無法喘息
塑料中的你很孤獨
傲慢得
如同女皇

曉波在大連獄中的三年
我每個月都咬著牙
走進你的領地
你帶著鋸齒的聲音
總是對我說
你不用再來了
我是他媽媽我會為他準備一切
對我從北京背來的東西
你不屑一顧

我無力使你柔軟
大海令我疲憊

Mother,
I know you never liked me.
All along you suspected I had planned
everything: your son imprisoned,
his refusal to live with you in Dalian,
and even your illnesses—
all my fault.
You couldn't stand my laugh.
You asked me to leave.

The first time I went to your house
it was full of plastic sheets and bags.
The sofa, mattress, carpet, heater, the drawers,
and even the cutting board and kettle
were covered or filled with plastic.
I couldn't breathe.
You looked lonely in your plastic house
but proud
as a queen.

Every month during the three years
when Xiaobo was in that Dalian prison,
I had to bite my tongue
to enter your territory.
Each time, with a sawtooth voice,
you said to me, "You don't need to come again.
I'm his mother. I will take care of everything."
As for the things I brought from Beijing—
you didn't bother to take a look.

I couldn't make you soft.
The ocean of Dalian wore me down.

在一年半的時間裡
我見不到曉波
只能低聲下氣
小心翼翼地詢問你
媽媽，曉波他現在怎麼樣
你說他瘦了
我就尋找各種有營養的食品
你說他臉腫的沒有了樣子
我就四處求醫問藥
你說他太胖了
我就寫信叮囑他
沖奶粉時不要再加方糖
在你的魔棒下
我發瘋地旋轉
你總是對的
我必須忍受你

我曾嘗試做個乖巧的兒媳
送你新衣服厚實的棉襪純金的手鍊
可這些東西被你
原封不動地棄置一旁
我請你外出吃飯，你說
有毒
你只不拒絕一樣東西
那就是我帶給你的藥
你喜歡吃藥
勝過世上所有的食物
而你的醬缸裡
長滿了蛆

For a year and half
I couldn't see Xiaobo,
so I asked you humbly
and cautiously,
"Mother, how is Xiaobo doing?"
You said he lost weight
so I tried to find nutritious foods.
You said his face was terribly swollen
so I sought medical advice from everywhere.
You said he was getting too fat
so I told him in a letter
not to add sugar when making powdered milk.
Under your magic wand
I moved around desperately.
You were always right,
and I had to tolerate you.

I tried to be a well-behaved daughter-in-law.
I gave you new clothes, cotton socks,
and gold bracelets, but you put them aside,
unopened.
When I offered to take you out to eat, you said
the food was poisoned.
There was one thing you didn't reject,
the medicine I brought you.
You liked taking medicine
more than any food in the world.
Your pickled veggie pot
was full of worms.

媽媽
那麼多的塑料布隔絕了我們
對同一個男人的愛
離間了我們
我們無法相互靠近
在我們最應該相互安慰的日子裡
我們成為敵人

有一天探監回來
你自言自語
讓曉波他死掉算了
從那一刻起
我不再掩飾對你的仇恨
你是魔鬼, 媽媽

你終於去了
那些塑料袋子被徹底丟棄
我不乞求和解
然而, 陰影裡
你時隱時現
曉波在睡夢中被你驚醒
無助地呻吟
你忘記帶走的假牙
正在咬噬我
讓我難以確定
這到底是不是個好的結尾

媽媽
請不要擋住
照亮我筆尖的這束光
讓這些文字活下去
請允許我念完
《為死者祈禱》

2/13/2001

Mother,
so many plastic sheets separated us.
Love for the same man
split us apart.
We couldn't get close to each other.
When we needed each other's comfort
we became enemies.

One day you came back from the prison
and talked to yourself:
"Let Xiaobo die. Done with it."
From that moment on I didn't
need to hide my hate.
Devil, mother.

You are finally gone.
Those plastic bags are in the trash.
I don't pray for reconciliation,
but you appear regularly
in the shadows.
Xiaobo was startled by you in his dreams—
you were moaning helplessly.
You've forgotten to take your dentures
which are biting me,
making me doubt
if this is the right ending.

Mother,
please do not block the light
that illuminates my pen.
Let these words survive.
Let me finish reading
"Praying for the Dead."

2/13/2001

瘋語

我是一個名叫尼金斯基的人的身體裡的靈魂
我吃得很少，儘管我很瘦
我只吃神讓我吃的東西
我討厭鼓脹的腸子
那會阻礙我跳舞

我害怕人群
害怕在他們前面跳舞
他們要我跳歡娛的舞蹈
歡娛就是死亡
他們感覺不到
卻要我過和他們一樣的生活

我要留在家裡
避開人群
把自己關在房間裡
望著天花板和牆壁
監禁中我也能找到生命

我是不思想的哲學家
是生命的劇場
不是虛構
我是有身體的神
喜歡用詩來談話
我就是韻律

安眠藥不能讓我入睡
酒也不能
我越來越累
我想停下來
但神不允許

Rant

I'm the soul in the body of Nijinsky.
Gaunt, I eat little, only
what the gods allow me.
I hate having a bloated
stomach. It inhibits dancing.

I'm afraid of crowds,
of dancing for them—
they demand a joyful jig
but joy is death. They feel
nothing but want
my life to match theirs.

I stay home to avoid
the crowds. Shutting
myself up in a room,
I stare at the walls and ceiling
to feel a life in this prison.

I'm a philosopher who thinks
with my body,
I'm biological theater,
nonfiction, the body
of spirit whose language is
poetry. I am prosody.

Sleeping pills don't work,
and alcohol doesn't work either.
I'm exhausted and want
to stop, but this spirit in me
won't permit it.

我要一直走
走到很高的地方往下俯視
感覺我所能到達的高度
我要走

2003

I need to go, to go
to some great height and look down.
I need to go until I reach that height
I need to go.

2003

無題

——給曉波

你說話你說話你說實話
你白天說夜晚說只要醒著就說
你說呀說
你在封閉的房間裡你的聲音衝到外面擴散
二十年前的那場死亡重又回來
來了又去如同時間
你缺少了很多東西但亡靈們與你同在
你沒有了日常生活加入亡靈們的呼喊
沒有回答沒有

你說話你說話你說實話
你白天說夜晚說只要醒著就說
你說呀說
你在封閉的房間裡你的聲音衝到外面擴散
二十年前那個傷口還在流血
鮮紅鮮紅如同生命
你喜歡很多東西但更愛與亡靈們為伴
你對他們承諾與他們一起尋找真相
路上沒有燈光沒有

Untitled

—for Xiaobo

You speak and speak and speak the truth.
You speak day and night, as long as you're awake
you speak and speak.
Your voice breaks free from the sealed room and disperses.
Death from twenty years ago returns—
it comes and goes like time.
You've lost many things, but the dead spirits are with you,
you give up your daily life to join their shouts and cries,
but there is no answer. None.

You speak and speak and speak the truth.
You speak day and night, as long as you're awake
you speak and speak.
Your voice breaks free from the sealed room and disperses.
The wound from twenty years ago still bleeds—
bright red, resembling life.
You like many things but prefer to accompany spirits,
you promise to seek the truth with them
but there is no light on the path. None.

你說話你說話你說實話
你白天說夜晚說只要醒著就說
你說呀說
你在封閉的房間裡你的聲音衝到外面擴散
二十年前槍聲決定了你的生命
永遠活在死亡裡
你愛妳的妻子但更驕傲她與你共度的黑暗時間
你讓她隨心所欲更堅持讓她死後繼續給你寫詩
那些詩行沒有聲音沒有

9/4/2009

You speak and speak and speak the truth.
You speak day and night, as long as you're awake
you speak and speak.
Your voice breaks free from the sealed room and disperses.
The gunfire from twenty years ago still drives your life—
you live forever in death.
You love your wife and are proud she stays with you
through the darkness; you let her do what she wants, write for you
even after death, but in her verses there are no sounds. None.

9/4/2009

碎片8

我常常注視讀到過的
死亡之光
覺得溫暖
為不得不離開感到悲哀
我想去有光的地方

多年來保持的頑強
變成了塵埃
一棵樹
一陣閃電就可以將其摧毀
什麼都不想

未來對我而言
是一扇關閉的窗戶
窗內的夜晚沒有盡頭
噩夢從沒有消失

我想去有光的地方

2011

Fragment No. 8

I often look at the light
from death
and feel warmth, then loss
when I must leave the page.
I want to go where there's light.

My strength, worked for years,
has become dust. A tree
can be destroyed
by lightning,
leaving nothing else to want.

For me the future is
a closed window
where night has no end
and nightmares can't be lifted.

I want to go where there's light.

2011

無話可說

鄰家婦人終日坐在院子裡
望著眼前的景物
沒有人知道原因
到了晚上或下雨時
女兒會扶她進屋
有時女兒忘了或不存在
這婦人就在院子裡待一整夜
無論天氣如何
一動不動

附近的人說
這婦人曾愛過一個男人
生下了他的孩子
那男人失蹤之後
她變成了瘋子
戰爭過去了
人們一連幾天沒有看到
鄰居婦人出現在院子裡
她的女兒也不見蹤影

黑暗中
鄰居婦人雙手長時間
放在臉上
女兒躺在床上
光著身子
睫毛緊閉

Nothing to Say

The woman who lives next door sits
in the courtyard all day, staring straight
ahead. No one knows why.
At night or when it rains
a daughter might help her in.
If the daughter forgets or doesn't exist,
the woman might stay in the yard
all night, motionless
regardless of weather.

Neighbors say
this woman loved a man,
had his child and,
after he went missing,
she went mad.
Now the war is over.
No one has seen her
in the yard for days.
The daughter, too, has disappeared.

In the dark
the woman holds her hands to her face
for a long time,
the daughter lies in bed
naked,
eyes closed tight.

最終, 屋中的一場大火
結束了一切
這是她唯一可以容忍的方式

廢墟上的天空
太陽光很亮

11/16/2011

In the end, the house catches on fire
finishing it all.
That's the only ending she can tolerate.

Above the ruins
the sunlight is blaring.

11/16/2011

大雪

——給劉暉44歲生日

弟弟，今天是你的生日
農曆大雪
我打開一瓶紅酒
想着送什麼禮物給你
好像抱抱你

給你也擺上個酒杯
我們倆喝喝酒，聊聊天
你曾經給我過生日的照片
就在眼前
那天的我們大笑着

沒有你的家裏
一切都變得扭曲
老爸一天比一天沉默
把你的兒子當成了你
老媽哭壞了眼睛
你的兒子遠走異國他鄉
老哥忙得腳不黏地
你的姐夫每個月都會問起你
而我時常夢到你
夢中的你一直在和我吵架
做我的弟弟很辛苦吧

Snow

—for Liu Hui's 44th birthday

It's your birthday today, little brother,
the Day of Great Snow on the lunar calendar.
I open a bottle of wine
and think about what gift I'd give you
as a form of embrace.

I set a glass out for you.
Let's drink, the two of us, and chat.
Once you gave me a photograph for my birthday—
it's right here—
a day we were both laughing.

Without you, our home
is distorted.
Daily, father becomes quieter,
mistakes your son for you.
Mother cries her eyes dry.
Now, your son is off in a foreign land.
Our big brother is busy; his feet hover above the floor.
Your brother-in-law asks about you every month,
and I dream of you all the time.
In my dream you quarrel with me—
it must be hard to be my brother.

還記得一九七六年的夏天
唐山大地震後
我們一起坐綠皮火車去長沙
火車開動時
不敢告訴你
第一次離開家
我心裏有多害怕

如果有可能，弟弟
現在請你以小時候的心態
無條件信任我
一切都會過去
火車總會到達終點

12/7/2013

I remember the summer of 1976.
After the earthquake in Tangshan
we went to Changsha on a green train.
When the train started,
I was afraid to tell you
how frightened I was
to leave home for the first time.

If possible, brother,
trust me now, unconditionally,
like when you were a small child,
that this will be over soon—
our train will reach the final station.

12/7/2013

抄經

沒日沒夜
我抄經
金剛般若波羅蜜經
我要趕在冬天之前
趕在樹葉落光之前
用心抄下每一個字
送給溫暖我的朋友

沒日沒夜
我抄經
金剛般若波羅蜜經
可冬天還是來得太快了
大風颳走了樹木的衣服
不知道因為什麼
朋友們悄無聲息地遠去了

沒日沒夜
我抄經
金剛般若波羅蜜經
字迹愈來愈端正
證明我還沒有徹底瘋掉
我畫中的樹
長不出一片葉子

12/2013

I Copy the Scriptures

Day and night,
I copy the Diamond Sutra
of Prajnaparamita.
Before winter comes, before the leaves fall
completely, I want to finish writing
every word with my heart at attention,
for my friends who have given me warmth.

Day and night,
I copy the Diamond Sutra
of Prajnaparamita.
But winter has come too soon.
Wind has blown away the trees' clothes.
I don't know why
my friends are gone, quiet.

Day and night,
I copy the Diamond Sutra
of Prajnaparamita.
My writing looks more and more square.
It proves that I have not gone entirely
insane, but the tree I drew
hasn't grown a leaf.

12/2013

站立

這是一棵樹嗎?
這是我一個人
這是冬天的樹嗎?
它一年四季都是這個樣
葉子呢?
葉子在視線以外
為什麼畫樹呢?
喜歡它站立的姿勢
做樹活一輩子很累吧?
累也要站著
沒有人來陪伴你嗎?
有鳥兒啊
看不到鳥呀
聽那翅膀飛舞的聲音
在樹上畫鳥會很好看吧?
我又老又瞎看不到了
你根本不會畫鳥吧?
是的我不會
你是棵又老又笨的樹
我是

12/12/2013

How It Stands

Is it a tree?
It's me, alone.
Is it a winter tree?
It's always like this, all year round.
Where are the leaves?
The leaves are farther away.
Why draw a tree?
I like how it stands.
Aren't you tired of being a tree your whole life?
Even when exhausted, I want to stand.
Is there anyone to keep you company?
There are birds.
I don't see any.
Listen to the sound of fluttering wings.
Wouldn't it look nice to draw birds in the tree?
I'm so old and blind I wouldn't see them.
You don't know how to draw a bird, do you?
You're right. I don't know how.
You're an old, foolish tree.
I am.

12/12/2013

Translators' Afterword

When translating a poet, there is often an empty chair. Wouldn't it be nice, when unsure of how to render a line or a word, to sit down with the poet you are translating and ask her how to proceed (even though her suggestions would probably complicate matters further)? When translating a poet who is no longer living, the desire to interact with the poet can be productive. It creates a longing that fuels going back to the work again and again to feel the presence of the author, her words reaching out. But in the case of Liu Xia, the empty chair feels different. The desire to reach out to her feels devastating as Liu Xia has been under house arrest in Beijing since 2010 and is more or less cut off from the world, from us.

Yet, the desire to sit in the same room as Liu Xia, to discuss her work with her, fuels the work too, albeit in a different way than when translating someone from another time. We are fueled by Liu Xia's absence to make her work as alive and potent as it is in the original Chinese so that her absence becomes a presence. We want her readers to feel the weight of her silence through her powerful voice. We want her readers to long to sit with her as we do, to see how, in conversation, she might transform desperation for a different kind of life into humor as she does in her work. To see how she might critique someone while showing understanding. Liu Xia's poems are at home with waiting and with chaos and are sheared by entrapment; she sees her imprisonment brutally, sometimes through the clarity of narrative and sometimes through the disturbing lens of surreal imagery.

Who wouldn't want to sit with her, to learn how to keep seeing, to keep looking within silence?

Liu Xia's love for a human rights activist was her political crime, and so for her there can be no love poem that is not a political poem. Love is not just love, it is staking a claim against the present political situation. Home also means prison. For translators, the interweaving of referents, of the personal and political, of the daily and of the national, can feel difficult, and can highlight the silence. But, despite the multivalence in her work, Liu Xia's poems feel conversational, like a mind open to sorting things through out loud, to telling stories with others listening around a table.

And so our process in translating the work mirrored the work itself. We translated the poems in conversation with each other. Ming Di is a Chinese poet living in the United States and Jennifer Stern is an American poet who has lived in China. Ming Di draws on her sensitivity to the ways Liu Xia's work rings out in the original and sees the work in the context of Chinese poetry, while Jennifer Stern draws on the daily experience of interpreting Chinese language and culture from an American perspective, and places Liu Xia's translations in the context of English language poetry, hearing how English might hold the power of the Chinese originals. Together, we talk through a way to remain true to impossibly collapsed dichotomies, to a person who we feel like we know but don't. We have tried to remain true to what we value in the work, to what's rooted in the gutted and stark political present in China, and in the loving, friendly, funny, insightful, and engaged voice.

Liu Xia is always writing ahead of her time, always outside of the current moment or beyond it. Perhaps this is why her work reads as timeless. Liu Xia wrote strange yet down-to-earth narratives in the 1980s and yet it wasn't until the 1990s that poets Xiao Kaiyu, Zhang Shuguang, and Sun Wenbo started promoting narrative poetry. From 1976 to 1986, "Misty" poetry was the most prominent school or trend in China which was influenced by Western poetry through translation and was marked by a lofty tone, grandiose lyricism, and rebellious gestures against the government. Liu Xia's poetry was distinctively different in those years; hers was grounded in the small things, in interiority; her poems lived in the world of daily life. Post-Misty and Third Generation poets emerged in the mid 1980s, and they promoted local "spoken language" rather than the written language and "foreign" sounding style in the Misty poetry. Although Liu Xia became known after the publication of her poetry and fiction in 1982 and continued publishing until 1989, she didn't belong to any popular circles. From early on, she draws inspiration and strength from fiction writing, and blends storytelling and poetry to recreate folktales, a hallmark of her writing in the 1980s. Confessional poetry was popular among the women poets in China in the 1980s and early 1990s, which came to them by way of translations of American confessional poetry. Although Liu Xia admires Sylvia Plath, her work never reads as confessional.

After the failure of the June 4th movement in 1989, there was a moment of silence, most of the Misty poets went into exile abroad, and then new voices in poetry emerged. Some poets were drawn to narrative; some wrote poems of controlled emotion with a touch of satire, with subtle imagery deployed to avoid censorship. Again, Liu Xia went her own way, taking from the poetics she knew and building a new way to write into this restrained and fraught terrain. She drew inspiration from artists and novelists such as Vincent van Gogh and Franz Kafka, but also explored words as objects, as worlds, and thus became more abstract.

From 1996 to 1999 when Liu Xiaobo was serving a three-year sentence, Liu Xia took many black-and-white photographs of dolls, "ugly babies" as she called them, as a way to communicate. She didn't want the prison guards to read her poetry, but she had much to say. Some of the photographs portray the lives of Chinese people during those years—those caged with no freedom, or silenced and suffocated by plastic, and those trying to escape, challenging the system by daring actions, or protesting at the door of the imperial palace now occupied by the government. Other photographs present a more personal and private sphere, such as the two "ugly babies" imprisoned behind the bars of the empty chair. While Liu Xiaobo wrote to her from prison in passionate poems, she stayed calm in her writing, saying:

Living with dolls, the power
of silence is omnipresent.
The world opens in four directions,
and we communicate with gestures.

("Silent Strength," 1998)

Liu Xia, in her writing, gestures with all that poetry has to offer, with stories and reinvented legends. We hear the power of silence with recreations of stark absence. We see animals that seem human and humans who act otherwise. In this new century, her poems, which came to us through various channels, have further darkened, gone into obsession and the absurd, because, we sense, Liu Xia will write bravely into the darkest parts of poetry. She will go as far as she can with her words. We have tried our best to follow her.

We can't sit together, with Liu Xia, so we've sat together with her work, attempting to bring the poems into an English that creates a sense of absence, a political absence, through a potent presence. We hope that you will sit with her, until her silence is something we no longer need to abide.

We would like to express our gratitude to Jeffrey Yang for taking the time to read the entire manuscript and for providing many invaluable suggestions; to Liao Yiwu for making everything possible; to Tienchi Martin for her moral support; to Peter Bernstein for representing the author; to Liao Weitang for providing the Chinese edition of *Selected Poems of Liu Xiaobo and Liu Xia* (Xiafeier Press, Hong Kong, 2000); to Chinese PEN for making the first fifteen poems into a booklet and organizing a reading in New York with PEN America; to Herta Müller for her foreword; to Jeff Shotts and Graywolf Press for the support throughout the process of translation and for publishing this bilingual volume; and finally to Liu Xia for providing additional poems in Chinese, for her trust in our translation, and for her extraordinary work, vision, and art.

MING DI & JENNIFER STERN

Liu Xia is a Chinese poet and artist, born in 1961 and raised in Beijing. She started writing poetry and short stories in 1982 and published in major magazines such as *Poetry* and *People's Literature* in China, but she stopped publishing after the 1989 Tiananmen incident. She worked for the Beijing Tax Bureau until she quit work in 1993 to become an independent writer. Liu Xia has also made more than three hundred paintings, and since 1996 has devoted herself to the art of black-and-white photography. She met the writer and critic Liu Xiaobo in the early 1980s at a literary gathering; they married in 1996 while he was serving a prison sentence. Liu Xiaobo was first jailed from 1989 to 1991 due to his involvement with the June 4th student movement. He was detained without trial in 1995, then sentenced to a three-year imprisonment from 1996 to 1999. Because of his participation in drafting Charter 08, a pro-democracy manifesto, he was sentenced to an eleven-year prison term in 2008, which he is still serving. He was awarded the Nobel Peace Prize in 2010, at which time Liu Xia was placed under house arrest. She remains unable to leave her home and with very restricted contact with the outside world. *Selected Poems by Liu Xiaobo and Liu Xia* was published in Hong Kong in 2000, which was Liu Xia's only official publication after 1989. *The Silent Strength of Liu Xia,* an exhibition of her photographic work, traveled to several countries in her absence. *Empty Chairs: Selected Poems* includes her poetry over thirty years from 1983 to 2013.

Ming Di was born in China and lives in the United States as a poet and translator, author of six collections of poetry in Chinese and four volumes of translation. A selection of her poetry has been translated into English, titled *River Merchant's Wife* (Marick Press, 2012). She edited and co-translated *New Cathay: Contemporary Chinese Poetry* (Tupelo Press, copublished with the Poetry Foundation, 2013).

Jennifer Stern is the pen name for an American poet and translator who has published one volume of poetry in English. She has worked as an editor and has translated poetry from several languages.

The Lannan Translation Series
Funding the translation and publication of exceptional literary works

The Scattered Papers of Penelope by Katerina Anghelaki-Rooke, edited and translated from the Greek by Karen Van Dyck

The Last Brother by Nathacha Appanah, translated from the French by Geoffrey Strachan

The Accordionist's Son by Bernardo Atxaga, translated from the Spanish by Margaret Jull Costa

The Lovers of Algeria by Anouar Benmalek, translated from the French by Joanna Kilmartin

The Star of Algiers by Aziz Chouaki, translated from the French by Ros Schwartz and Lulu Norman

Before I Burn by Gaute Heivoll, translated from the Norwegian by Don Bartlett

Child Wonder by Roy Jacobsen, translated from the Norwegian by Don Bartlett with Don Shaw

A House at the Edge of Tears by Vénus Khoury-Ghata, translated from the French by Marilyn Hacker

Nettles by Vénus Khoury-Ghata, translated from the French by Marilyn Hacker

She Says by Vénus Khoury-Ghata, translated from the French by Marilyn Hacker

A Wake for the Living by Radmila Lazic, translated from the Serbian by Charles Simic

June Fourth Elegies by Liu Xiaobo, translated from the Chinese by Jeffrey Yang

No Shelter by Pura López-Colomé, translated from the Spanish by Forrest Gander

The Life of an Unknown Man by Andreï Makine, translated from the French by Geoffrey Strachan

New European Poets, edited by Wayne Miller and Kevin Prufer

Look There by Agi Mishol, translated from the Hebrew by Lisa Katz

Karate Chop by Dorthe Nors, translated from the Danish by Martin Aitken

Ashes in My Mouth, Sand in My Shoes by Per Petterson, translated from the Norwegian by Don Bartlett

I Curse the River of Time by Per Petterson, translated from the Norwegian by Charlotte Barslund with Per Petterson

I Refuse by Per Petterson, translated from the Norwegian by Don Bartlett

Out Stealing Horses by Per Petterson, translated from the Norwegian by Anne Born

To Siberia by Per Petterson, translated from the Norwegian by Anne Born

Tesla: A Portrait with Masks by Vladimir Pištalo, translated from the Serbian by Bogdan Rakić and John Jeffries

In Times of Fading Light by Eugen Ruge, translated from the German by Anthea Bell

Shyness and Dignity by Dag Solstad, translated from the Norwegian by Sverre Lyngstad

Meanwhile Take My Hand by Kirmen Uribe, translated from the Basque by Elizabeth Macklin

Without an Alphabet, Without a Face by Saadi Youssef, translated from the Arabic by Khaled Mattawa